OLD SOUL

22

OLD SOUL 22

YOU ARE NOT ALONE

QUAY BODDIE

TATE PUBLISHING
AND ENTERPRISES, LLC

Published by Tate Publishing & Enterprises, LLC
127 E. Trade Center Terrace | Mustang, Oklahoma 73064 USA
1.888.361.9473 | www.tatepublishing.com

Tate Publishing is committed to excellence in the publishing industry. The company reflects the philosophy established by the founders, based on Psalm 68:11,
"The Lord gave the word and great was the company of those who published it."

Published in the United States of America

ISBN: 978-1-63306-533-8
1. Religion / Devotional
1. Biography & Autobiography / Personal Memoirs
14.10.13

ACKNOWLEDGMENTS

IT MAY BE cliché but, I do want to Thank God for just allowing me this opportunity. I never in a million years would have imagined this happening but, it happened and I love it! Even though she is no longer with us anymore, I want to thank my grandmother Dorothy Boddie. She has instilled in me more than you will ever know. You want to know why I am the man I am today? She took the time out to make me into a man and I am more than greatful for that.

To my hometown, LaGrange, GA I can say that I am proud to be from such a great place. To my second home in Rome, GA and, my Shorter University family thank you for having my back and supporting me. To all of the coaches who have coached and believed in me, thank you. All of my family, close friends, old friends and, people I have built some sort of relationship with; thank you.

Everything I do is for you all and I mean that from the bottom of my heart. I hope that you enjoy these compilations. We are in this life together, you are not alone and, I love you forever.

CONTENTS

truly believe that, we are to motivate and encourage others in this life to push through no matter what and that's what I hope to accomplish through these compilations. To whoever is reading this book, you are not alone when it comes to going through, things. I like to think of myself as an encourager. I hope that this devotional will open up your eyes and let you know that whatever it is you are going through you will see the light soon.

ROLLER COASTER

Ups and downs, twist and turns, bumps and humps, fast pace, slow pace. You ask yourself, "How many more loops, when is the last turn, will this coaster break down?" But by the time all this goes on in your mind, you are on the final loop, coming in to get off. The point shows no matter what roller coaster you are on, God is the operator of it and he wants you to see that you will be safe and that he will protect you, he will help you overcome your fears, and he fights all of your battles. So, the next time you are looking for a roller coaster buddy, look next to you because God is always looking to ride with you.

> "Havent I not commanded you: be strong and courageous? Do not be afraid or discouraged, for the Lord your God is with you wherever you go (Joshua 1:9)."

THE FALL

THERE IS A slip, trip, and fall in your life a.k.a. (the mess up). The sad thing about it is you fall more than once in your life. The "slip" is having something in your mind that is not supposed to be there. You think you would try to get rid of it but that leads to the "trip." The "trip" is going to do that thing that you know is not good for you, but you still do it anyway. You know in your heart its going to hurt yourself as well as Jesus. The "fall" is actually commiting that displeasing thing that you had in your mind. All of these things could have been easily avoided, so why did you do it? We have to stop letting the enemy get the best of us. Nobody is perfect granted, but we still must be careful of what we think and do. We must realize that the slip, trip, and fall, will come about, but staying with God is what remains.

"Though a righteous man falls seven times,he will get up, but the wicked will stumble into ruin (Proverbs 24:16)."

THE ADVICE

I'm so repetitive when it comes to giving advice. People probably get tired of me saying what I say. You want to know something? I don't care if they get tired of it or not because I only know one name to mention when giving advice. Jesus, He is the Almighty, the one in charge, a provider, a friend, a healer, and if you let him he can be your everything. Now, do you see why I'm so repetitive, or do I need to remind you what he does for me and how he has changed my life? Open up to what he wants to do in your life. Let him change you from the inside and out and when someone asks you for advice, you can't help but to be repetitive like I am. Being repetitive in Christ is actually the best decision you could ever make in your life. Hopefully, what you begin to believe will rub off on others, and their mindset will then, too, be repetitive.

"We know that all things work together for the good of those who love God: those who are called according to his purpose (Romans 8:28)."

STORMS

YOUR LIFE WON'T always be a piece of cake everyday even though it that would be nice God told us that we would suffer. "When it rains, it pours" and sometimes, that can turn into a storm. Storms are horrible because there is not too much you can do but sit still and wait for it to be over. You never know when it's over until the rain stops and all calms down. Translation to our lives, when we are going through tough times; we may feel like we don't know what to do at all. The whole time, God is waiting for you to lay your burdens down to him. The second you do that, the wind, rain, and overall storm can be gone. He is the weatherman; if you want to know the forecast it comes from spending time with him. He can prepare you for storms, and when it's all said and done, you give him praise. Through it all, he will forever be the shelter from the "storm."

"We wait for the Lord; He is our help and shield (Psalm 33:20)."

DESIRES

STAYING FAITHFUL RESULTS in God giving you the desires of your heart. You probably think, Well when are my desires coming? God knows, and it's up to us to be patient and find out. It could be days, months, or even years, but you just have to hold on and have faith. As humans, we can sometimes desire a lot. I don't really desire alot or at least I dont think so. One thing that I really desire is a wife along with other things of course. Someone who is God-fearing, loving, caring, supportive, unselfish, and I want her to have humility. Someone I can call my own and have a family with one day "God willing". If you have desires and you want them to be fulfilled, then be all God wants you to be and watch it fall into place. No matter if your desire is to be married and have a family, accomplish certain goals, or whatever it may be, just sit tight it just may work in your favor.

To my wife, whoever you are, this is dedicated to you. I can't wait to spend the rest of my life with you. I pray for you daily, and I love you. I just wanted you to know.

If you really want something to make it happen, you have to believe it, pray it and see it. Watch it happen!

> "Take delight in the Lord, and he will give you your hearts desires (Psalm 37:4)."

TIGHT GRIP

FIRM LIKE A man's hand-shake. Clunge like a child to their mother. Holding on to what you believe in everyday. Fighting the world and its challenges. Maybe, before you were living in the world and your grip wasn't so tight, but now, you serve a purpose and a king. You have that tight grip, and you are not letting go. Let nobody loosen you up to where your grip starts to change. You have to realize that life (the rope) that you have a grip on can be what you make it. Its like tug of war daily; have that tight grip and dont let go.

> "So we must not get tired of doing good, for we will reap at the proper time if we don't give up (Galatians 6:9)."

TEST TIME

GOOD OR BAD situations happen all the time. You can sometimes feel when something is going to happen and sometimes you have no idea. In my opinion, God is testing us in these times. You say you love him and adore him. Well he is surely about to test you on that. Once you are of him and know his promises those situations should be easier to handle no matter what it is. There is nothing to big or small that God can't handle. There is nothing that we can do about what happens in our lives because we don't control it. So, I simply say situations are what you make them but just know you have to be strong no matter what.

> "If indeed you remain grounded and steadfast in the faith, and are not shifted away from the hope of the gospel that you heard. This gospel has been proclaimed in all creation under heaven, and I, Paul, have become a minister of it (Colossians 1:23)."

FORWARD MOTION

STOP RIGHT THERE! Don't take another step! Pause, reflect, and look at the life that you are living! You have either been stuck or backtracking for far too long. It's time for a change. It's time for something new and exciting. It's time for you! Forget the setbacks, heartbreaks, struggles, and pains because ultimately, you know what needs to take place. A past is called a past for a reason so leave it there. Where is your passion? Where is your motivation and ambition? Where is your drive?

> "Tear your hearts, not just your clothes, and return to the Lord your God. For He is gracious and compassionate, slow to anger, rich in faithful love, and he relents from sending disaster (Joel 2:13)."

THAT'S OKAY

DISRESPECT ME OR downgrade me I'll be fine. Hate me, taunt me; I will still be the same. Point out my flaws and make me look bad; it's cool. Laugh and poke fun at me; I'm still standing. You can-not and will not break me, but I applaud you for trying. After all, this is said and done, I will still love you because thats what I am told to do by God. It's easier said than done but we must obey. Whatever we have to do to please God, we should do whether we like it or not. So go ahead pick at me; do as you please. I'll just look at you and say, "That's Okay."

> "No weapon formed against you will succeed, and you will refute any accusation raised against you in court. This is the heritage of the Lord's servants, and their righteousness is from me (Isaiah 54:17)."

IMPROVEMENT

COMPARE YOUR CHRISTIAN walk to training for a sport. In the beginning, you are not as strong as you want to be because you have just started. Pain, soreness, and sometimes crazy and negative mindsets are trying to creep in. Before long, you get the hang of it and it's not so bad anymore. You are stronger, and your mindset is changing. You realize what you must do and how to do it. Now, here goes the doing part will you let pain, suffering, and heartache stop you from being the best you can be and improving at your sport. You may not be where you want to be but thank God you are not where you used to be. Training pain will enter the body, but at least you have Jesus to help you fight it.

> "Do not be conformed to this age, but be transformed by the renewing of your mind, so that you may discern what is good, pleasing, and perfect will of God (Romans 12:2)."

JOY

NOBODY CAN TAKE joy from you unless you let them. When Jesus came into your heart so did joy. Joy is what gets you through the tough times and trials. Life happens, events occur, and things won't always go your way. Does that mean you are going to let somebody take your joy away from , or are you going to keep your cool and press through?

> "In that day you will not ask me anything. I assure you: Anything you ask the father in my name, He will give you. Until now you have asked nothing in my name. Ask and you will receive, that your joy may be complete (John 16:23-24)."

LETTING DOWN

WALKING DOWN A road and not knowing when it will end. On this road , I think I am by myself. Maybe because at first I didn't know who was above, and I was blind and didn't know better. All of a sudden, like a child drowning in a pool, my father came and saved me. He now guides my life and everything I do. He is my all and all forever. When I am at my lowest, he is always there for me. No matter how stubborn we are he never lets us go or gives up on us. As humans, we can let others down or dissapoint others not on purpose, but it happens. One thing you never have to worry about is Jesus letting go. No matter what you do in your life his love is unfailing.

> "Finally, brethren, farewell. Be perfect, be of good comfort, be of one mind, live in peace; and the God of love and peace shall be with you. (2 Corinthians 13:11)."

LET 'EM KNOW

OBSTACLES COMING AND going "No problem." Trials and tribulations "I'll manage." Worry and doubt in my heart "you must be crazy." Jesus on my side "You better believe it." Let them know this is how you are everyday!

> "To him who alone doeth great wonders: for his mercy endureth for ever (Psalm 136:4)."

PIECES

Your life is like a puzzle, but the thing is we are not putting the pieces together; it's God who is doing that and knows exactly where the pieces go and when to put pieces down. When we try to put pieces together ourselves it ends up in disaster. Thank you, , for being the puzzle master.

> "For I know the thoughts that I think towards you, saith the Lord, thoughts of peace, and not of evil, to give you an expected end (Jeremiah 29:11)."

LIFE ROLES

You may have been born to play leading roles in your life or maybe you were menat to be a curtain closer. Either way, God loves you enough to let you be on the set of the show he runs. Don't think your life is worthless because God doesn't make mistakes.

> "Casting all your care upon him for he careth for you (1 Peter 5:7)."

TRASH

It's trash day! Whatever is keeping you from following God with your all is "trash." Yeah I said it! Guess what? I have trash in my life too, but its time to take that three- week old pizza (non sense) or that orange juice that expired (negative talk and lies) away. It's like the old folks say; you start to hang around trash, you will start to stink like it. Be fresh in Jesus not funky with the devil.

> "And he that sat upon the throne said, Behold, I make
> all things new. And he said unto me, Write: for these
> words are true and faithful (Revalations 21:5)."

THE SAME

WE ALWAYS LOOK left and right but never in front of ourselves to see that God is always there and does not move. He will always do and be the same person whether it's blessing you or him delivering you from something he has you in his hands.

> "Jesus Christ the same yesterday, and to day and forever (Hebrews 13:8)."

LIVE STRONG

THE ENEMY CAN'T take anything from you unless you let him. Oh yeah, sure he is going to try and get you down but remind him that there is a king in you, and he cannot and will not take away what God has given you. If you don't remember this, your life will be a mess but if you do remember this you can conquer any day that is given to you. Be happy, bless someone, tell somebody what God has done for you in your life.

> "He will keep the feet of his saints, and the wicked shall be silent in darkness; for by the strength shall no man prevail (1 Samuel 2:9)."

A WILL AND WANT TOO

IF YOU HAVE that drive and a desire for things to get better and do things in your life, you must have "a will and want too." Just sitting around waiting for something to happen will get you nowhere. I can't point the finger because I'm guilty too, but at the same time, remember " with God all things are possible". Nobody can ruin what God has already promised you but you.

> "Jesus said unto him, if thou canst believe, all things
> are possible to him that believeth (Mark 9:23)."

GOT YOUR BACK

I'LL PUT IT in war terms. If you had to be in a foxhole hiding from the enemy, wouldnt want Jesus in that hole with you? No weapon pulled on you will work or be effective. No crazy, lunatic can hold you down. They have already been defeated, and you have already won the war. Do you believe that?

> "Be not ye therefore like unto them: for your father knoweth what things ye have need of, before ye ask him (Matthew 6:8)."

REAL LOVE

I HOPE EVERYDAY for you or your significant other is always special. If you don't have a significant other, that is perfectly fine. Remember, all the love in the world can't compare to the love Jesus gives. We can expect that everyday.

> "As the father hath loved me, so I have loved you: continue ye in my love (John 15:9)."

IMPRESSION

I CAN REMEMBER an old coach, saying "Fellas, every game you play, there will be somebody new in the stands, watching you for the first time and that may be the last time they ever see you play. What kind of impression will you leave on that person? It's the same way with your daily walk you want people to know who you who you live for. Show them you have God in your life and make an impact in someone's life because it could be their last time ever seeing you again."

> "That ye might walk worthy of the Lord unto all pleasing, being fruitful in every good work, and increasing in the knowledge of God (Colossians 1:10)."

VICTORY

Everyday you wake up you have already won the day. Do you believe that? God wants more from you in this day. No matter what is going on in your life, at the moment know that you have won. Since you have won today, if tomorrow, comes you can win that too. Don't let life beat you, "You beat life". Letting life beat you is a trick from the enemy. The winner in you comes from the best coach of all time- Jesus!

> "But thanks be to God, which giveth us the victory through our Lord Jesus Christ (1 Corinthians 15:57)."

SHOCK THEM

BE A SURPRISE to the people that are around you by how you respond to things going on in your life. It's sad to say but some want to see you go off the deep end and just lay down. Show them that you are a warrior. Someone with a fighting attitude who never throws in the towel will continue to shock the world.

> "For we are made partakers of Christ, if we hold the beginning of our confidence stedfast unto the end (Hebrews 3:14)."

ALWAYS NOT JUST SOMETIMES

You don't just stay strong and stay upright for yourself when things are all good. You stay strong for the people that you love and for the people that look up to you. If you are down about something, the people you love will also be that way. Release off positive energy never negative. People are watching you and admire you whether you know it or not.

> "Thy shoes shall be iron and brass; and as thy days, so shall thy strength be (Deuteronomy 33:25)."

PUSH

PUSH FORWARD, AND don't be focused on trying to pull back that may not be in God's will for you right now. Pushing forward is going towards your blessing the only way pulling back can be recaptured again is if God shows you and brings it back to you otherwise leave it alone. Easier said than done, but it can be done. Push. (Pray until something happens)

> "Rejoicing in hope; patient in tribulation; continuing instant in prayer (Romans 12:12)."

ROAD BLOCK

Road block- designed to get you off your course of travel for a certain period of time. Road blocks are simply trails, tribulations, or hardships that happen in your life. Will you let these road blocks stop you for longer than you had expected, or will you overcome it and the enemy? Keep it moving! Keep your head up!

> "Now unto him that is able to keep you from falling, and to present you faultless before the presence of his glory with exceeding joy (Jude 1:24)."

FOUNDATION

WHAT DO YOU come from? Growing up was life good for you or was it rough? Were you the outcast or just like everybody else? No matter what or where you come from a foundation in your life must be solid. Foundations can come from whatever you take in your life as value. God, a certain way you were raised, etc. are the things that have probably kept you grounded. If your life is not where you want it to be, then you might want to peep into what your foundation is like. Don't put blame on where you are from, what you grew up doing, what you are involved in. You change you! You revamp your focus! You stay in tune with the foundation that is set for you!

> "But we all, with open face beholding as in a glass the glory of the lord, are changed into the same image from glory to glory, even as by the spirit of the Lord (2 Corinthians 3:18)."

PURSUIT

WHAT ARE YOU going after? I mean something must drive you and motivate you in your life, or at least I hope. You first have to see it happening. You have to say it. You have to then do it. Who can stop you once you have your mind made up? Your mindset should be, Nobody can stop me but me. Once you show and prove that you were serious to those who doubted, then there comes the "I told you so"! Now, thats pursuit!

> "But seek ye first the kingdom of God, and his righteousness; and all these things shall be added unto you (Matthew 6:33)."

ALL ABOARD

THINK OF YOUR life as a train you board that God is the conductor of. So many trains but yet so many are going in different directions. We all have different destinations we all have certain points that we will reach. We all have passengers that may even want to load your train with you. You may have some that don't want any part of your train at all. What I'm really trying to say is that let anybody spoil your ride. Either they will enjoy the trip with you or they won't. As long as God controls the train and you are on it then, how can the ride be ruined? The passengers that once claimed they wanted to be on your train have just missed out. All aboard!

> "Remember ye not the former things, neither consider the things of old. Behold, I will do a new thing; now it shall spring forth; shall ye not know it? I will even make a way in the wilderness, and rivers in the desert (Isaiah 43:18-19)."

BLINK OF AN EYE

THEY SAY YOU can't do it. They say you won't do it. They say there is no way ever possible. What are you believing in? Are you believing in yourself or what they have to say? People can talk all day long, but what they don't know is what's inside of you. A fighter, a competitor, a champion, a stallion, a warrior that has not yet been exposed. My daddy used to say, "Just wait, when you least expect it im coming for you". When the nay-sayers come against you, they have no idea what they have gotten themselves into. In the blink of an eye, you will be on top and all will ask how. Your reply will be, "Never blink on my hustle".

> "I can do all things through christ which strengtheneth me (Phillipians 4:13)."